A COLLECTION OF PHOTOGRAPHS
OF MARTIN LUTHER KING, JR.

A LASTING IMPRESSION

A COLLECTION OF PHOTOGRAPHS OF MARTIN LUTHER KING, JR.

by Hermene D. Hartman
With a foreword by the Reverend Jesse L. Jackson

Photographs by John Tweedle

PUBLISHING ASSOCIATES, INC.   1996

Copyright ©Publishing Associates, Inc. 1996

Dr. King's quotations from "The Un-Christian Christian," *Ebony* Magazine (Johnson Publishing Company, Inc.) August 1965. Reprinted by permission of Joan Daves. Copyright ©1965 by the estate of Martin Luther King, Jr.

Published in Atlanta, Georgia by Publishing Associates, Inc.

FIRST EDITION published in 1983 by the University of South Carolina Press, Columbia, South Carolina. ISBN: 0-87249-431-4

SECOND EDITION published in 1996 by Publishing Associates, Inc. 5020 Montcalm Drive, S.W. Atlanta, Georgia 30331

All rights reserved. No part of this book may be reproduced in any form, by mimeograph or any other means, without permission in writing from the publisher.

Manufactured in the United States of America
ISBN: 0-942683-25-0

Library of Congress Cataloging In Publication number
C.I.P. : 96 - 85979

To Mrs. Coretta Scott King, widow of Martin; and Mrs. Dianne Tweedle, widow of John; and their children Yolanda, Martin Luther III, Dexter, and Bernice King; and Miisha Tweedle and Sydney Vasquez.

This book is also dedicated to the many who felt inspired and compelled to join in the non-violent Civil Rights Movement insisting that America be accountable to all its citizens.

CONTENTS

ACKNOWLEDGEMENTS   ix
PREFACE *by Hermene D. Hartman*   xi
FOREWORD *by the Reverend Jesse L. Jackson*   xv
JOHN TWEEDLE *by John White and Hermene D. Hartman*   xix

A LASTING IMPRESSION

A COLLECTION OF PHOTOGRAPHS
OF MARTIN LUTHER KING, JR.   1

ACKNOWLEDGEMENTS

This book was not so much written as it was compiled, with me acting as producer. People who knew and loved either Dr. Martin Luther King, Jr. or John Tweedle gathered the material and supplied the information.

My loving appreciation to the Reverend David M. Wallace who knew about this project when John and I first discussed it. He was supportive and encouraging. I am thankful also to the Reverend Edgar Riddick. Dave and Ed have been walking history books. During Dr. King's Chicago visit they were young men establishing their careers. Both were influenced by King; both worked with John Tweedle. They were gracious as they relived those years, recalling dates, times, places, and events. They brought the story alive by sharing significant information about their own lives.

Dianne Tweedle, John's widow, has been a tremendous resource as we worked together to bring attention to the work of her husband and through that work to keep him alive for their daughter, Miisha.

Two of John's protégés, Michelle V. Agins and Victor Powell, worked with Dianne and me in preparing this book. Victor, who apprenticed with John during his last years, provided the initial working prints for the book and constantly reminded us which photos of Dr. King were significant to John. Michelle, who has followed John's path in becoming the personal photographer of the Chicago Mayor, Harold Washington, printed all the photographs in this book from John's negatives. She tried to print "in the Tweedle style," so that the resulting pictures seem as though he had printed them himself. And thanks to Robert Serbins for technical assistance and consultation in reproducing the photographs.

This book could not have been put together without the assistance of Evyette Jones. She visited Chicago newspapers, libraries, and historical societies for the printed material on Dr. King's years in Chicago. Evyette patiently read documents and made valuable suggestions sometimes simply by raising questions on a history she had learned orally. Thanks for helping me pull the pieces together.

We are particularly grateful to Faith Christmas and Fred Sengstacke of the *Chicago Daily Defender* newspaper for their personal interest in helping us tell a story. Karen McCormic, Public Service Representative, of the *Chicago Sun-Times* was especially considerate uncovering sources of King data.

Sara Pitzer at the University of South Carolina Press has been overwhelming in her commitment to this project. My sincere thanks to all of you for helping me make this dream a reality.

— HERMENE D. HARTMAN

PREFACE
by Hermene D. Hartman

Martin Luther King, Jr. influenced my life in three stages; as a child, as a teen and as an adult. I was still in high school when Dr. King came to Chicago, but his activities had had an effect on my thinking even when I was in grammar school and he was in Birmingham, Alabama. We were studying civics in school, learning about the Declaration of Independence and the Constitution, and I couldn't understand the paradox between what we were learning and what I saw on television when I went home at night. I'll never forget the feeling I got when I saw dogs being released on demonstrators and water being forced on freedom marchers. In school I kept asking, "If we have natural rights, why are our people being bitten by dogs? If we are all created equal, why are firehoses being turned on our people?" And the teacher couldn't answer. At the time I thought he didn't see the paradox because he didn't know the answer. I didn't understand that he *couldn't* answer. It was very confusing and I asked the same questions over and over. The Constitution said very clearly that we all had equal rights but what I saw on television happening during the demonstrations showed it was not true. So I wondered if the Constitution was wrong. I kept asking, the way a little kid does, "Who's lying?" And at home I asked my parents, "If such things happen in the South, could they happen in Chicago? Do we need something like that here?" Dr. King had created a stirring, an awakening in me.

When Dr. King came to Chicago I wanted to march. My mother thought it would be dangerous. People probably would get hurt and some would go to jail. I didn't march. I wasn't afraid of the possible violence but I had to respect the feelings of my mother. Instead, I joined with the other Black students in my high school (there were eleven Blacks in a school of six hundred and twenty-five) and we carried signs in the halls between classes. We didn't miss any classes. We left a couple of them early to carry our signs, but we went everywhere we were supposed to be, and the rest of the time we walked up and down those halls with our signs.

Later my mother learned about Jesse Jackson's activities with Operation Breadbasket, which was the Chicago arm of Dr. King's Southern Christian Leadership Conference (SCLC), located on 47th Street on the South Side. Being a teenager, I was unwilling to give up school dances and such for something as seemingly insignificant as licking envelopes. Three years later, when Dr. King was killed, I went through a period of guilt about not having been involved. I thought, "I could have done something and I didn't."

I started going to the Saturday morning Breadbasket meetings that were held in the Parkway Ballroom on 45th Street. The meetings were attended by a cross-section of the community and among those were a little girl and her great grandmother whom I met there every week. Later I learned that the lady was Jesse's grandmother, Mrs. Matilda Burns (we call her Tibby) and Jesse's oldest daughter, Sandy.

The meetings were a form of community socializing, often accompanied by gospel-jazz music. But the main focus was the fiery sermons of Jesse Jackson and others.

These ministers talked differently than anyone I had ever heard. They generated such excitement. They preached about love, justice, and power, but what they said had more substance than just preaching. The Bible became a living story rather than an historical narrative. Jesus became an activist rather than a simple historical figure. These movement ministers told the audience how to bring about social change in a nonviolent way and provided a continuation of Dr. King's militant interpretation of Jesus.

I was very shy at the time, but I went up to Jesse after one of those meetings and volunteered to help. He introduced me to the Reverend Willie Barrow, who coordinated direct action activities and engaged at that time in a boycott of food chains unfair to blacks.

I went to the offices every day after school for an entire week. Too shy to ask what they wanted me to do, I just sat there. Finally I found Jesse and in frustration said, "I've been sitting here one week and I haven't done one thing. I came to help not sit." He replied, "Speak up. You have to let them know you're here." I started typing, doing clerical jobs and anything that needed to be done. Many of my friends wondered at me; not understanding that it was a commitment.

By this time I was attending Roosevelt University and studying political science. I combined the theory taught in school with the reality found at Breadbasket. David Wallace, Edgar Riddick, Gary Massoni, and James Bevel helped develop my concepts of social ethics and theology. I also learned much from other volunteers, people like Richard Thomas, Noah Robinson, Michael Knighten, St. Clair Booker, Lucille Conway Loman, the Reverend Calvin Morris, Larry Shaw, Cirilo McSween, Jack Finley, Leon Davis, Paul Walker, Al Johnson, George O'Hare, Jerry Bell, Al Robinson, Roberta Jackson, Dr. Alvin Pitcher and Jo Ella Stevenson. It was from these people I learned how to work and the work never stopped. I worked first with the Reverend Ed Riddick doing research, and then I started working with the Reverend Dave Wallace in the communications department. Here I met John Tweedle. He was the director-producer of a show called "Our People," on WTTW-TV. At the time he was the only Black television producer in town, and working with John and David I learned the basics of mass media communications.

I began to understand the need for developing positive Black images. We developed a trade fair and cultural "Black Expo" to promote Black businesses We began Black parades for Christmas and Easter with new symbols, such as, the Black Saint and the Black Lamb.

During those years we had what we called Workers Council, which met on Friday evenings. They were really leadership meetings, though no one called them that, and they went on for hours. Jesse lectured to about twenty of us about how to put our philosophy into action. He talked about strategies in boycotts, about how to get candidates elected, how to demonstrate effectively. He talked about issues. He talked about social justice. In essence, he presented a problem, an analysis and a solution. It balanced what I was doing in college. There we talked about the principles of the Federalist Papers, John Locke, Plato, Thomas Jefferson, and so on; then with Jesse we talked about Mayor Richard J. Daley and precinct captains. It was the theoretical contrasted with the practical; the history with the contemporary. All the while we were working to make change happen. My sense of values was maturing and I was learning how to take a project from its initial idea and work it through implementation to realization.

I learned that one person *could* do something. Working with those young militant ministers who wore jeans rather than three-piece success suits, I developed a sense that what I did mattered. I saw that ideas, concepts, and dreams could become realities if people worked on them in the right ways.

I remember the day Nelson Rockefeller, who was running for the presidential nomination, came to the South Side of Chicago and to our dinky little office to have his picture taken shaking hands with Jesse. This added a dimension to my understanding of power.

In a real sense, even as they have traveled different paths, Dr. King's lieutenants have had a ripple effect, shaping the persuasion of another generation. Dr. King's impact is beyond measure. We are still a long way from his dream of social justice and equal rights. We have much more work to do before bigotry and prejudice will be subjugated. But, he left us with a nonviolent but militant method. He made a lasting impression on people who were never in his presence.

He questioned his country's morality and sense of social justice and forced the country to reflect painfully. He changed Black America's self-concept.

He captivated people, influencing lives as they developed their own postures. He nurtured his students to become leaders in their own quest and even when they went their separate ways, they have persisted in his principles and teachings. He led leaders. He gave our people the power of dignity. He was a profound man in a profane world.

NEW PREFACE: A LASTING IMPRESSION, 1996
by Hermene Hartman

A Lasting Impression, originally published in 1983 by the University of South Carolina Press, served as an historical, pictorial document of Dr. Martin Luther King Jr.'s visit to Chicago to help secure open housing rights and improve overcrowded, segregated public schools. The photographs of that visit were never published before. They are the work – the art – of the late John Tweedle, who became the first Black photojournalist to work for a major metropolitan newspaper, the now defunct *Chicago Daily News*.

The photos contained herein have become more precious as the years have passed. They record a critical juncture in the American Civil Rights Movement – when Dr. King first brought his strategy of non-violent direct action protest out of the racist South to employ it in the racist North. This collection includes photographs of Dr. King's address at Soldier's Field, July 10, 1966, where he spoke before an assemblage of nearly 100,000 people. It is nearly 30 years to the day that this new edition of *A Lasting Impression* is published. Dr. King's visit set the stage for the rise of independent politics in Chicago and paved the way for Harold Washington's historic rise to the office of Mayor in 1983.

Much has changed since *A Lasting Impression* was published in 1983. John Tweedle, a very skilled and lovable man, has passed, as has the Rev. Edgar Riddick, a researcher for the National Offices of Operation Breadbasket, who was instrumental in the publishing of this book. Dianne Tweedle, John's widow, continues in service to the community today in the management of residential properties in Chicago. John's daughter Miisha is married to Oscar Vasquez and they have one daughter, Sydney.

I have changed careers, moving from being a college professor in behavioral sciences to publisher of *N'DIGO*, a "magapaper for the urbane" geared to Chicago's Black middle-class. John Tweedle introduced me to the profession of mass media communications.

Martin Luther King, Jr.'s deeds and life work, which served as a benchmark for progress in Black America, are threatened now, as we watch the clock on Affirmative Action and other gains of the Civil Rights Movement being turned back. There have been many significant national mood shifts resulting from Dr. King's mission. Rev. Jesse Jackson, Jr., a Dr. King aide, launched two successful presidential bids, representing the consolidation of Dr. King's most significant achievement, ensuring the right to vote for African-Americans. Countless state and national political offices are now held by African-Americans.

Andrew Young has continued the King legacy as U.S. Ambassador, Mayor of Atlanta, Georgia, and Chairman of the Atlanta Committee for the Olympic Games (ACOG). John L. Lewis is currently U.S. Representative (D-GA), and a chief advocate for the quality of life for all people. And there have been many others.

We have seen Nelson Mandela released from prison to become South Africa's President and watched Black South Africans stand in line for hours to vote in their first election ever. At the same time, voters in America have become increasingly apathetic.

Finally, this book is special. Not many document King's moods and activities on the street as he interacted, marched and lived, as this volume does. Not many discuss King's northern experience. John clearly realized that his photographs of Dr. King were a camera shot of history in the making!

FOREWORD

Dr. Martin Luther King, Jr. *A Recollection*

By The Reverend Jesse L. Jackson

Everywhere he went and in everyone he touched there was change. He changed the image Americans had of Black heroes. Until this time Black heroes were limited to athletes and entertainers. As a young Baptist minister, Dr. King became a new kind of Black hero. He was a conqueror.

He changed me. As a young person growing up in Greenville, South Carolina, I was raised indirectly under his influence. At fourteen I became a student of the Civil Rights Movement. For the first time in this country the sense of Black revolt was so strong in the air that you could feel it. A non-violent revolution had begun. My direct involvement with this twentieth century prophet began the spring of 1965, when students and faculty of the seminary I attended responded to the crisis in Selma, Alabama. I soon found the man I came to call "Doc" was a wonderful teacher. He gave concise answers to my most complex questions. He made materialism seem infantile. He drove a Chevy. A station wagon has been my car. He taught me that the mission was more important than a vehicle. His wealth was in character, not things.

He changed the South. His journey began humbly and accidentally in December of 1955 in Montgomery, Alabama, when a tired seamstress, Mrs. Rosa Parks, refused to sit in her traditional place — the back of the bus. The twenty-six-year old minister was chosen by local Negro leaders to head what was to become a 383-day bus boycott that produced a Supreme Court decision making segregation illegal. It changed the course of history.

Dr. King applied the teaching of civil disobedience he had learned from the work of Mohandas Ghandi as a method to confront racism. His search for justice marked the decade of the sixties as a period of social chaos and consciousness raising. It was the beginning of an era Dr. King called "America's third revolution — the Negro Revolution." His organization, the Southern Christian Leadership Conference (SCLC), was formally organized in January 1957. He traveled throughout the South, with sit-ins, freedom rides, voter registration drives, marches, and selective buying campaigns to develop a New South. His Southern endeavors placed him in jail thirty times, usually with his partner, the Reverend Ralph Abernathy.

He changed the awareness of white clergymen. During his thirteenth jailing he wrote, "A Letter from Birmingham Jail," addressed to white clergymen, expressing the innermost feelings of Black Americans.

He changed the country's awareness of social injustice toward Black people. On August 28, 1963, he led the march on Washington. A quarter of a million Americans assembled in mass to support President John F. Kennedy's civil rights legislation. It was on this hot summer day Dr. King first said to the world, "I have a dream." King's theology was not about living to go to heaven or hell. He was an action minister expounding the social gospel. He was about the business of truth and love. He did not preach of death's redemption. He taught the transformation of a living situation. Because he raised questions, because he dared to care, because he accepted the challenge posed by Jesus, because he planted seeds, we bear his fruit to this day.

Because his organization, the Southern Christian Leadership Conference, led a voter's registration drive in Cleveland, the Honorable Carl Stokes was elected the first Black mayor of a major United States city in 1967. Because he raised issues of urban rot in Chicago in 1965, in 1983 the nation's second largest city has a Black mayor—Harold Washington.

He changed the North. In 1965, Dr. King decided it was time to come North to highlight that Northern racism was more concealed than in the South but still very much alive. He narrowed the choices to New York and Chicago, cities representing the nation's largest Black populations. SCLC staff people concluded New York's Harlem was too disorganized and fragmented. They chose Chicago, the hub of America's Black life. It was mecca for Black enterprise. Its political activity was unprecedented, and it had an effective political machine which could effect change. Its cultural life was rich. And Chicago had strong support from the religious community, Protestant and Roman Catholic, for civil rights efforts. The second largest city in the country had within it all the difficult problems faced by every other Northern city. As Andy Young, then executive director of SCLC said, "If Northern problems can be solved there they can be solved anywhere."

The pillars of Chicago's Black community — Edwin "Bill" Berry, Executive Director of the Urban League; Attorney Earl Dickerson; and the publisher, John H. Johnson, welcomed Dr. King. Albert Raby, convenor of a conglomerate of community groups, the Coordinating Council of Community Organizations (CCCO), extended the formal invitation to Dr. King.

So, he and his people chose the city discovered by a Black man—Jean Baptiste Pointe DuSable. The lakeside city with a beautiful skyline and a magnificent mile is where Dr. King's Northern Movement focused. The city was in for revolution.

During that period, I attended Chicago Theological Seminary, along with David M. Wallace and Gary Massoni. We three pioneered Chicago's Operation Breadbasket. In our last year of school, our lives were changed directly by Dr.

King's visit to Chicago. Dr. Alvin Pitcher, our ethics professor, helped us organize a minister's meeting held on Wednesday evenings, where we discussed social justice concepts. The Reverends Frank Sims, A.L. James, Clay Evans, Edmund Blaire, Stroy Freeman, the Reverends Claude and Addie Wyatt and Henry Hardy belonged to this group. As the ministers internalized these new ideas and impressions, their social attitudes and ministries changed. Not all accepted that. One minister became so disturbed by our thrust that he chased us out of the church with a loaded gun. And the Reverend Mr. Evans was severely penalized for his association with us. His new church building, Fellowship Baptist Church, stood unfinished for seven years because some politicians claimed he violated city building codes and his bank loan was held up.

It was in these conditions, in the heat of resistance, that the Chicago Chapter of Operation Breadbasket was born. We organized in 1966. We met on Saturday mornings. Our goal was to use the power of the Church to produce employment and business opportunities for Blacks. What began as an internship became a life's work. Neither David nor I returned to the seminary. On Christmas Day in 1971, Operation Breadbasket was transformed to Operation PUSH (People United to Save Humanity) and our first meeting was held in the Metropolitan Theatre, the "Met," just steps away from where the original Breadbasket offices were housed with CCCO on 47th Street, right off South Parkway. Since then, Saturday morning meetings have become a force that cannot be ignored. Local and national leaders have sought this platform to make important announcements and deliver major addresses.

When Dr. King assigned Dave and me to raise funds, we realized quickly that the more we could increase business and employment opportunities for the Black community, the more successful our fundraising efforts would be. Jobs, justice, and economic development became our campaign goals. Black businesses increased their targets from thousands to millions of dollars. Business reciprocity was significant to the Black community; it had a direct effect on the quality of life.

Such activity allowed me to be creative. I was promoted from Local Chapter Director to Northern Director, to National Director Operation Breadbasket

Dr. King's move to Chicago redefined the city. King was seen as a direct threat by the late Mayor Richard Daley, whose throne was shaken. The power political machine was troubled. Suddenly, orderly, obedient Negroes became socially chaotic. The city was becoming dismantled. For the first time in Daley's regime, where he ruled as Democratic Party king, another King trod. They locked into a heated power struggle. Marches, demonstrations, protests, rallies were daily occurences.

Marches into communities like Marquette Park and Gage Park became a part of Chicago's bloody history. Dr. King commented after he was hit in the head with a rock from the Gage Park open housing march that it had never been so bad in the Deep South. During the Gage Park demonstration, cars were overturned and burned, and policemen attacked from tree tops. Midwesterners were attacking a Nobel Peace prize winner on their front lawns. The urban jungle had exploded. Daley painted Dr. King as a "troublemaker." He tried to punish him, his workers and his supporters. Daley lost. He played short-range politics. Dr. King won. His strategy had long-range implications. He was planting seeds for social change. Plantation politics was dying. A new breed of politician was being conceived.

Ours is an extension of Martin's work. The natural evolution, the logical conclusion, of the civil rights revolution is in politics. Many other of Doc's people are there, including Andrew Young and Walter Fauntroy. In the fifties we raised the question of Blacks' right to vote; in the eighties we raise the question of the right to be President of the United States. Dr. King struggled for freedom; as a free people, we struggle for equality.

It is difficult to fit the man we called "Doc" into historical context. His life defies definition. He means so much to so many. He was Black America's first mass leader. He changed our minds about ourselves. He gave us psychological independence. He ended legal apartheid in America. Some have compared his life to Christ's, and it is true, life for Black Americans can be divided into two major eras: BK – Before King and AK – After King. He redefined the struggle, giving us a positive method for overcoming a negative situation, giving us successful means by which the least of us could fight.

This mild mannered man had a unique ability to articulate our groans. His message exceeded the race question; its essence dealt with love, power, and justice. He took Black America into the arena of global politics. As he interacted and related to power, he forced the world to view us with respect.

His legacy is he challenged a nation to succeed, to support its codes of ethics, to obey its own creed of conduct. He made America behave democratically.

He was martyred a young man, only 39, with many of his personal dreams yet to be realized. He didn't live to see his own four children grow to adolescence. He didn't live to see his disciples mature as leaders in their own disciplines. But his life was so full it could not be contained by a grave. He lives today in the changes he began. Martin did not make an annual contribution to the cause of freedom. He did not belong to the benefit banquet circuit. His life was devoted to liberation for his people. He made the ultimate sacrifice and we are the benefactors.

This is a better country today because of a Negro preacher's caring character.

JOHN TWEEDLE
July 5, 1936-December 8, 1981

Photography is an art. Photojournalism is art with generous amounts of intelligence, guts, sensitivity, dedication, compassion, mother wit, patience, stick-to-itiveness, technical skill, oomph, and much more mixed in. To understand John Tweedle, one has to realize that he had all these ingredients and more.

A photojournalist must be in tune with life; Tweedle was in tune with the spirit of life itself. He was a visual communicator who tapped the intrinsic values of life; he was a visual historian.

That old saying "never a dull moment"—that was true of Tweedle. He was like Santa Claus with no suit, just a camera, but always jolly. And he was tough, no one pushed him around. And no one ever went hungry around him; the food was always first class. He was flying above the dark clouds of life.

I first heard of John Tweedle at a photography seminar at the University of North Carolina at Chapel Hill. The speaker, Chuck Scott from the *Chicago Daily News*, talked about how great the city was and how great the paper.

"But," I asked, "are there any Blacks on the staff?"

There was a long pause, his head dropped, his voice changed, and Chuck told of being at the annual Chicago Press Photographers' Awards dinner a few months earlier.

Sitting at the head table was John Tweedle, who was to be honored as the first Black on a major Chicago newspaper. Just as the awards were being announced, a message was rushed up to the speaker.

"We have just received word, Dr. King was killed moments ago..."

Chuck told us how Tweedle dropped his head on the table and cried uncontrollably. And he told us how important John Tweedle was as a Black and as a visual communicator.

When I arrived in Chicago, Tweedle gave me a big brother welcome on the telephone and told me what he was going to do to me if I didn't start shooting great pictures, continuing the pace he had set. His call was a big surprise and a great challenge.

Before the week was over, I was covering a riot on Chicago's South Side from an unsafe position between the cops and the rioters. This big guy came over like a football player running interference, directing me to a safer location where I could still record the event. Tweedle became an instant coach-quarterback.

He was physically big and used it to his advantage in many situations, but it was balanced by that pleasant, childlike personality. He was caring.

Tweedle liked being around me; he was proud and happy for others to make it. He enjoyed being a team player and always played the big brother role. Black pride flowed through his veins. He gloried in being Black. He wanted others to know Blacks were working on major dailies. He got together a collection of my pictures and I became a guest on his TV show, my first Chicago TV appearance.

We laughed a lot together and shared many hours discussing personal issues, the world and Black responsibilities to society, and our foreparents; and many hours practicing our skills, attacking situations with the camera.

Tweedle was deeply aware of visual impact. His great eye, excellent skills, endless energy, and his ability to see and feel the whole scene enabled him to capture many angles of an event. He was a master of the technical. He enjoyed life's entire studio.

He always said that from events the mind retains images, visual images captured on film and then preserved not only in the photographic anthologies of the day but in the minds of millions who beheld them. And in this day of sophisticated journalism, where the written word is more critically prepared than ever before, and where live television takes us to events as they happen, it is still the frozen moment of photojournalism that is the mainstay of our memories.

Tweedle's camera was his passport to history. He truly lived the spirit of photojournalism. He understood lights and light, people and nature. He used his gift of sharing and giving something extra to life. He believed that where excellence is a daily habit, vision grows and his camera became an extension of his eye, heart and body.

His images are imprinted upon not only photographic paper but upon hearts and minds. He, too, had a dream: to share in book form what he saw and felt, with and for others — visual impressions of life. He knew that dreams come true and that seeds planted in rich soil produce good fruit. It's good to see this book, for those impressions will continue to be a part of us.

Tweedle and I always talked about winning a Pulitzer. It was December 8, 1981, following a meeting with my editors about my entry that I walked over to the photo desk, feeling a chill, knowing there was a touching story in the air. I was told that Tweedle had just died.

At first I felt lost, hurt, empty, but knowing Tweedle, he would have said, "Just keep on keeping on…"

I thought of his spirit of life and of living, his oomph for recording and sharing what he saw and felt and I felt a new challenge — like being handed a torch during a race. I thought of what a blessing it was to have worked with him. I remember during one of our last conversations, I'd said, "John, big brother, when I grow up, I'm gonna be like you."

And he just smiled…

JOHN H. WHITE — 1982 Pulitzer Prize winner
Chicago Sun-Times Photographer

John Tweedle was a robust, jovial man. He never had to say, "smile," as he snapped the shutter. You looked into his round face and automatically responded that way. His human qualities represented the very best of living and loving.

John was a photographer's photographer. Many photographers could take pictures of the same event but people always wanted John's pictures. He saw things, moments, and events with a very special eye. John was the first Black photo-journalist hired by a major daily newspaper. He worked for the *Chicago Daily News* from 1964 to 1968 and rejoined the staff in 1974 where he remained until the paper ceased publication in 1978. Tweedle paved the way for many other people in the media, particularly photojournalists, two of whom have since won the Pulitzer Prize.

John's life was photography; rarely did you see him without his camera. He did not take pictures. He recorded moments. He documented time. He captured a spirit.

Tweedle was a master communicator. He earned degrees in Media Communications and advance degrees in Communications Science. He was a producer-director at Chicago's Public Television Station, WTTW-TV. Again, he was the first Black in Chicago to hold such a position.

When the Civil Rights Movement came to Chicago, John became its unofficial official visual recorder. On every major effort, at every event, he was there with his camera. He knew that the action was more than exciting, that there was history in the activity. He was aware and sensitive to the nuances of events as he delicately documented King's Chicago year.

Of his work he said, "If a photograph is to be effective it must immediately communicate a feeling or idea." John's wife, Dianne expressed his attitude this way, "John expressed many sides of life as he saw them. He followed as few rules as possible always believing that his love and instinct would guide him. He went for the picture that grabbed you in a vital spot and any vital spot would do. He believed a picture was graphically balanced when it moved you."

Perhaps the proper description of John is that he was a poetic photographer. Shooting just for fun one summer day, he caught former Mayor Michael Bilandic jogging on Chicago's lakefront. The photo appeared in *Newsweek*. Bilandic told John it was the best photo ever taken of him and asked if John would be his personal photographer. John did so, remaining at city hall until his untimely death.

This book reflects John Tweedle's vision and his unique sense of things happening about him. In this sense this photographic chronicle is as much about John as it is King. His photos speak to the sensitivity of shooting and the magic of the moment in the Movement. These are not staged, posed, studio pictures. They are recordings of a public figure working.

For years John and I had planned to prepare a book and an exhibit based on his photographs of Dr. King. We both sensed it was an important project. For five years, doing it was our New Year's resolution. Because we discussed the idea so often, I knew his favorite prints, all of which appear in the book. There are thousands of negatives; I have been through them hundreds of times. It has been difficult to choose which belonged. My final selections have been those photos which show Dr. King's many moods and represent the best quality from John's lens.

John Tweedle died of a sudden, massive coronary while at work in Chicago's City Hall, December 8, 1981. He was talking to his wife on the telephone about attending a Christmas party. He died with his cameras on.

In this book we have finally realized our New Year's resolution and through it the spirits of John Tweedle and Dr. Martin Luther King, Jr. live.

HERMENE D. HARTMAN

A LASTING IMPRESSION
A COLLECTION OF PHOTOGRAPHS OF MARTIN LUTHER KING, JR.

To commemorate the silver anniversary of *Look* Magazine, January 1962, the editors requested world figures to make predictions for the next quarter of a century.

"By 1987, I would expect the Christian era to begin. Not because a balance of terror will have paralyzed mankind, but because most of the world's people will have realized that non-violence in the nuclear age was life's last chance."

Dr. King appears at a press conference on welfare rights.
With *(left to right)* Bill Wiley, Executive Director of
National Welfare Rights Organization, unidentified woman,
and the Reverends Ralph Abernathy and Al Sampson, aides.

One Sunday afternoon in March of 1965, leaving Liberty Baptist Church 49th and South Parkway, after having addressed a crowd of 5000 at the morning services in the church of his friend the Reverend A. Patterson Jackson, Dr. King stopped a motorcade of cars to greet a young child. Watching the scene, a woman brought her little girl to the car to meet Dr. King.

Chicago's City Council officially renamed the famous South Side Street, South Parkway, to Dr. Martin Luther King Drive on July 31, 1968.

On January 26, 1966, Dr. King and his wife Coretta moved into a slum on Chicago's west side to dramatize housing problems and urban decay. The North Lawndale apartment was a three-flight walkup and rented for $90 a month. Immediately after they moved in, the building was improved with painting, sanitation, and other surface changes. After this and protests, organization of tenant unions, marches, rallies, and rent strikes in Chicago, open housing became a reality.

Dr. King came to Chicago to raise the issue of slum housing. He and his aides arrive to view his new home. To his right are Meredith Gilbert, Stoney Cook, and Fred C. Bennette, Jr.

The Reverend Bernard Lee and the Reverend Edgar Riddick conduct a tour of the neighborhood.

Meredith Gilbert, director of the Lawndale Freedom Movement, with Dr. King.

Dr. King inspects his new Chicago west side apartment.

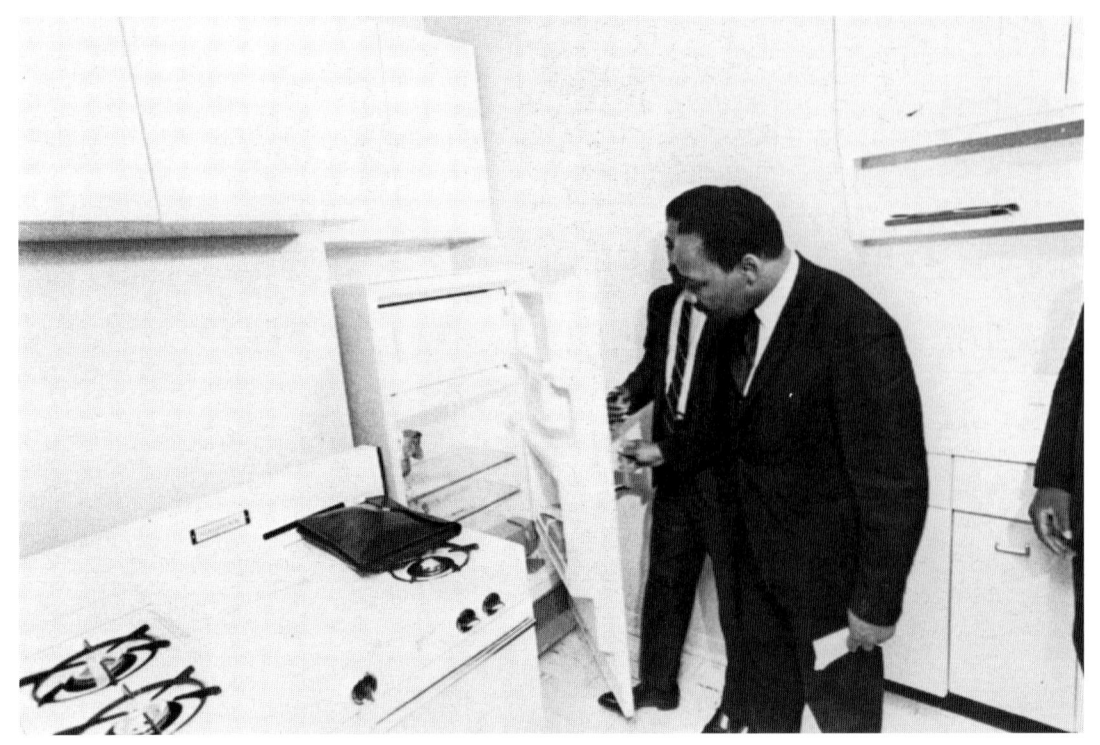

12

Dr. and Mrs. King receiving first guests.

Kids from the neighborhood stop in to say welcome.

Dr. King and the press walk Hamlin Street.

The back yard.

When people heard he was there, they came in mass. His move into the West Side slum attracted national attention.

The summer of '66 was besieged with demonstrations. Housing was a primary issue. People picketed in downtown Chicago, at the Real Estate Board Building.

Dr. King's protégés gathered in the rain for a "pray-in" on Chicago housing. Here *(left to right)* are Albert Raby, the Reverends Fred Shuttlesworth, Jesse Jackson and James Bevel.

Rallies were held in churches throughout the city
to bring an end to slums. He listened and he spoke.

SOLDIER FIELD RALLY

On Sunday, July 10, 1966, a "Freedom Rally" was held at Chicago's largest stadium—Soldier Field. The rally was sponsored by Dr. King's Southern Christian Leadership Conference (SCLC) and the Coordinating Council of Community Organizations (CCUO) headed by Albert Raby. CCUO consisted of over forty-four Chicago civil rights, religious, business, labor and neighborhood organizations. The two groups merged to become recognized as the Chicago Freedom Movement.

July 10th was a hot, blistering day. Junius Griffin, coordinator of the rally estimated the crowd at 65,000. They listened quietly as King spoke: "This day we must decide that our votes will decide who will be the mayor of Chicago."

He issued an emancipation proclamation to include thirty-five demands. After the rally, the huge crowd marched to City Hall and in the fashion of Martin Luther, founder of the German Evangelical Church and Protestant Reformation, posted a scroll on City Hall's main door, listing goals to make Chicago a racially open city. King's program included buying only from those firms that did not discriminate, keeping count of Black employees in business and public agencies, increasing the city's minimum hourly wage, demanding an open occupancy statement by public officials, seeking nondiscriminatory lending practices, and revoking city contracts with firms that lacked fair employment policies, desegregating Chicago public schools during the 1966–67 school year, creating a citizens' board to review police complaints, and replacing of absentee precinct campaigns in ghetto wards. A primary goal of the Chicago Freedom Movement was ending the city's housing discrimination. Dr. King said, "We must decide to fill up the jails of Chicago, if necessary, in order to end slums."

Stressing the importance of nonviolence, he said, "We must affirm that we will withdraw economic support from any company that will not provide on-the-job training and employ an adequate number of Negroes, Puerto Ricans, and other ethnic minorities in the higher paying jobs."

The summer of 1966 proved to be long and hot. The city exploded. Chicago became a changed city as a result of Dr. King's visit.

One of the community organizations participating in the Soldier Field rally was The Woodlawn Organization.

Approaching the stage with Dr. King are *(left to right)* Ed Chandler, Executive Director, Church Federation of Chicago; and Edwin C. Berry, Executive Director of the Chicago Urban League.

Rally organizers confer: *(left to right)* Dr. King, the Reverends Arthur Brazier, Stroy Freeman, and Bill Berry.

Dr. King and one of his favorite singers—Mahalia Jackson. Other entertainers to perform that day included Dick Gregory, Oscar Brown, Jr., and Stevie Wonder.

As he addressed the largest civil rights rally ever held in Chicago, he spoke on human rights: "We must make full and constructive use of the freedom we already possess. Many doors of opportunity are opening to the young people today that were not open to our mothers and fathers."

Following the speech, a handshake.

This was a familiar sight in the Movement. The typical closing of a meeting was to stand hand over hand and sing the hymn "We Shall Overcome."

After the rally, the crowd marched to City Hall.

In his memoirs, the late Senator Paul H. Douglas, renowned as a liberal, recalled that in the summer of 1966 the issue of open housing cost him his Senate seat. The Reverend James Bevel, chief of staff for Dr. King, determined to turn both Blacks and Whites against Democratic party candidates, including Douglas. Bevel vowed to march until every white man in the area (Gage Park) voted Republican. Douglas wrote, "That the influence of the Martin Luther King group should be used to aid my opponent was one of the baffling turns in the campaign."

Dr. King's reception in Chicago was mixed, even among the Black population. Some prominent citizens, including the Black aldermen known as "The Silent Six," said leadership in Chicago was competent to work out the city's destiny without his visit. They formed the Chicago Conference to fulfill these rights. It was chaired by the late Alderman Ralph H. Metcalf and Bishop Louis H. Ford, pastor of the St. Paul Church of God in Christ. Both men were from the South Side. In contrast, Dr. King received the active support of the Catholic Interracial Council of Chicago.

Harry Belafonte   Dick Gregory   Stevie Wonder   Oscar Brown Jr.

Harry Belafonte, humorist Dick Gregory, entertainer Stevie Wonder and folk singer Oscar Brown Jr. provided entertainment for Dr. King fundraisers in Chicago.

"The people downtown understand power. We must get their attention. Blacks and Whites are in this struggle together, we need our White friends. Tension is not between White and Negro, but between justice and injustice."

MARTIN LUTHER KING
Tuesday, July 27, 1965
Chicago Daily Defender

"I am many things to many people; Civil Rights leader, agitator, trouble-maker, and orator, but in the quiet recess of my heart, I am fundamentally a clergyman, a Baptist preacher. This is my being and my heritage for I am also the son of a Baptist preacher, the grandson of a Baptist preacher and the great grandson of a Baptist preacher."

MARTIN LUTHER KING, JR.
"The Un-Christian Christian"
Ebony Magazine (Johnson Publishing Company, Inc.), August 1965

Dr. King and his aide, the Reverend Jesse Jackson, leave the First Presbyterian Church in Chicago. At the time Jackson was a student at Chicago Theological Seminary.

Dr. King listens to Jesse with the Reverend John Thurston and Rosie Simpson.

Jackson listens to his mentor. The Reverend David Wallace adjusts microphone.

A group of young leaders *(left to right)* Albert Raby, the Reverends King, Andrew Young, and Walter Fauntroy. Some of the men with King have since become Congressmen.

Albert Raby extended the invitation to Dr. King to come to Chicago. He convened the Coordinating Council of Community Organizations (CCUO). Some years later, he was the campaign manager for Mayor Harold Washington, Chicago's first Black mayor.

Andrew Young listens as Dr. King addresses an audience. Listening was a future Congressman from Georgia, Ambassador to the United Nations, and Mayor of Atlanta, King's hometown.

Dr. King's closest friend was the Reverend Ralph David Abernathy, vice-president and treasurer of SCLC. He was one of the Movement's most gifted speakers. He was with Dr. King to the end.

"How can you advocate breaking some laws and obeying others? The answer lies in the fact that there are two types of laws; just and unjust. I would be the first to advocate obeying just laws. One has not only a legal but a moral responsibility to obey just laws. Conversely, one has a moral responsibility to disobey unjust laws. I would agree with St. Augustine that 'an unjust law is no law at all.'

"Now, what is the difference between the two? How does one determine whether a law is just or unjust? A just law is a man-made code that squares with the moral law or the law of God. An unjust law is a code that is out of harmony with the moral law."

MARTIN LUTHER KING, JR.
Letter from Birmingham Jail
April 16, 1963

The Reverend Archibald Carey and Dr. King in the Quinn Chapel African Methodist Episcopal Church. This is the oldest Black church in Chicago. The photo is in the Provident Medical Center Art Collection, Chicago.

Dr. King was a religious scholar—a social philosopher addressing the complexities of his day. He followed the gospel according to the Scripture, as unorthodox in modern times as Jesus was in His. The world was his church, the streets and stadiums his pulpits. He lived his life in worship.

"What has happened too often is that men have responded to Christ emotionally, but they have not responded to His teachings morally. The notion of a personal savior who has died for us has a great deal of appeal, but too often Christians tend to see the Resurrected Christ, and ignore the man Jesus, turning his face to Jerusalem and deliberately accepting crucifixion rather than deny God's will, and give in to the pressures of the Scribes and Pharisees to take back much of what He had taught concerning all men as sons of God."

MARTIN LUTHER KING, JR.
"The Un-Christian Christian"
Ebony Magazine (Johnson Publishing
Company, Inc.), August, 1965

Dr. King was murdered on Friday, April 4, 1968 in Memphis, Tennessee.

"I would challenge you today to see that his spirit never dies and that we will go forward from this experience which to me represents the crucifixion—on toward the resurrection and redemption of his spirit.

"We must carry on…"

CORETTA SCOTT KING
The Chicago Courier
January 11, 1975

THE PHOTOGRAPHER—John Tweedle

John Tweedle considered himself the "unofficial official visual recorder" of the Civil Rights Movement in Chicago. He photographed Dr. King at every major event during King's visit to that city. Tweedle was the first Black photographer to work for a major metropolitan newspaper, the *Chicago Daily News*. After the paper's demise in 1978, he joined the staff at City Hall in Chicago as the personal photographer of the mayor, Michael Bilandic. Tweedle served in that position until his untimely death in December 1981.

THE EDITOR – Hermene Hartman

Hermene Hartman is a distinguished participant of the Civil Rights Movement, an accomplished educator and a media pioneer, one of the few Black women in publishing.

She founded *N'DIGO* Magapaper, in 1989, and it has become Chicago's leading African-American publication. As a writer she is known for her publisher's page which provides hard hitting social commentaries on contemporary issues. *N'DIGO* is an alternative journal focusing on cutting-edge personalities, news profiles and topics of interests to the progressive segment of Chicago's Black middle-class.

Hartman's move to publishing came after her tenure as Vice Chancellor of the City Colleges of Chicago, where she headed the Department of External Affairs. The first woman to be named vice chancellor in the nation's second largest community college system, Hartman was responsible for media and community relations, as well as marketing and publications. It was during this tenure that she recognized the need for a venue representing a new view of contemporary culture.

Hartman, who has successfully operated The Hartman Group, a full-service public relations firm since 1977, taught behavioral sciences in the City Colleges system from 1973-'84, and previously produced public service programming for WBBM-TV in Chicago.

Her career began in the tumultuous, but stirring, years of the Civil Rights Movement. While finishing college, she was swept into the Movement by Rev. Jesse Jackson's Operation Breadbasket now Operation PUSH organization. Hartman coordinated the cultural segment of three annual PUSH Expos, which became America's largest international exhibition featuring Black artists.

Hartman holds Master's Degrees in Sociology and Philosophy of Education and recently completed an M.B.A. at the University of Illinois.

She is the daughter of the Herman Hartman, (deceased) the first Black Pepsi-Cola distributor in the United States, and Mildred Bowden, retired administrator at Cook County Hospital and the niece of the late jazz vocalist Johnny Hartman.